In Mem

Poems of Be

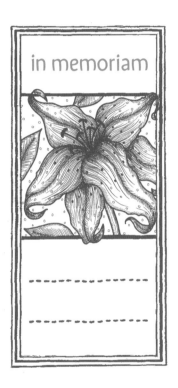

in memoriam

Candlestick Press

Introduction

Many extraordinary and important poems have been written about death and bereavement – the death of the old and the young, of a beloved parent, child, sibling, friend. The poems in this pamphlet honour the dead and acknowledge the mystery of our lives. They have been chosen for their clarity and beauty, and in the hope that they might offer consolation to the bereaved and also be helpful for people arranging a funeral.

Poetry is read at funerals in many traditions and cultures. It seems a natural way to remember the dead. The poems in this selection are a mix of the well-known and the less familiar, of the traditional and modern. Sometimes a small, quiet poem that nobody has heard before can touch us and speak to us more clearly than one that has become over-used and somehow ceased to mean anything personal.

All the poems are about the poet's experience of bereavement and mourning or meditations about death. Many are about death at the end of a long, rewarding life while others are about death coming suddenly and prematurely. The poems in the last few pages have the heart-break of a child's death as their subject.

Shared in public or read in private, poetry can put its arms around us all. As Jackie Kay writes:

> The dead don't go till you do, loved ones.
> The dead are still here holding our hands.

We hope that these poems, too, will hold your hand.

Carol Ann Duffy

"...the innumerable air kisses
we exchanged in passing
remain suspended to this day,
each one an efficacious blessing."

Christopher Reid, from **'Lucinda's Way'**

Remember

Remember me when I am gone away,
   Gone far away into the silent land;
   When you can no more hold me by the hand,
Nor I half turn to go yet turning stay.
Remember me when no more day by day
   You tell me of our future that you planned:
   Only remember me; you understand
It will be late to counsel then or pray.
Yet if you should forget me for a while
   And afterwards remember, do not grieve:
   For if the darkness and corruption leave
   A vestige of the thoughts that once I had,
Better by far you should forget and smile
   Than that you should remember and be sad.

Christina Rossetti (1830 – 1894)

Wanderer's Night-Song

O'er all the hilltops is quiet now,
In all the tree-tops hearest thou
Hardly a breath;

The birds are asleep in the trees;
Wait, wait - soon like these
Thou too shalt rest,
Thou too shalt rest.

Translated from Johann Wolfgang von Goethe (1749 – 1832)
by Henry Wadsworth Longfellow (1807 – 1882)

'don't tell me that I mourn too much'

don't tell me that I mourn too much
and I won't tell you that you mourn too much
don't tell me that I mourn too little
and I won't tell you that you mourn too little
don't tell me that I mourn in the wrong place
and I won't tell you that you mourn in the wrong place
don't tell me that I mourn at the wrong time
and I won't tell you that you mourn at the wrong time
don't tell me that I mourn in the wrong way
and I won't tell you that you mourn in the wrong way

I may get it wrong, I will get it wrong, I have got it wrong
but don't tell me.

Michael Rosen

The Dead

The dead are always looking down on us, they say,
while we are putting on our shoes or making a sandwich,
they are looking down through the glass-bottom boats of
  heaven
as they row themselves slowly through eternity.

They watch the tops of our heads moving below on earth,
and when we lie down in a field or on a couch,
drugged perhaps by the hum of a warm afternoon,
they think we are looking back at them,

which makes them lift their oars and fall silent
and wait, like parents, for us to close our eyes.

Billy Collins

The Baton

How smoothly you handed on the baton.
As if you'd known the time and place
and kept it secret from us; then
when the moment came, yielded it up
saying *Take it, quick, I cannot hold it,*
and let it swiftly slip your grasp.
We were left looking down at your empty hands,
the worn, surrendered fingers,
and a weight that had suddenly shifted.

Anna Wigley

Cold

It felt so cold, the snowball which wept in my hands,
and when I rolled it along in the snow, it grew
till I could sit on it, looking back at the house,
where it was cold when I woke in my room, the windows
blind with ice, my breath undressing itself on the air.
Cold, too, embracing the torso of snow which I lifted up
in my arms to build a snowman, my toes, burning, cold
in my winter boots; my mother's voice calling me in
from the cold. And her hands were cold from peeling
and pooling potatoes into a bowl, stooping to cup
her daughter's face, a kiss for both cold cheeks, my cold nose.
But nothing so cold as the February night I opened the door
in the Chapel of Rest where my mother lay, neither young, nor
  old,
where my lips, returning her kiss to her brow, knew the meaning
  of cold.

Carol Ann Duffy

from An Exequy

The rooms and days we wandered through
Shrink in my mind to one – there you
Lie quite absorbed by peace – the calm
Which life could not provide is balm
In death. Unseen by me, you look
Past bed and stairs and half-read book
Eternally upon your home,
The end of pain, the left alone.
I have no friend, or intercessor,
No psychopomp or true confessor
But only you who know my heart
In every cramped and devious part –
Then take my hand and lead me out,
The sky is overcast by doubt,
The time has come, I listen for
Your words of comfort at the door,
O guide me through the shoals of fear –
'Fürchte dich nicht, ich bin bei dir.'*

Peter Porter (1929 – 2010)

*'Don't be afraid, I am with you'

And Death Shall Have No Dominion

And death shall have no dominion.
Dead men naked they shall be one
With the man in the wind and the west moon;
When their bones are picked clean and the clean bones gone,
They shall have stars at elbow and foot;
Though they go mad they shall be sane,
Though they sink through the sea they shall rise again;
Though lovers be lost love shall not;
And death shall have no dominion.

And death shall have no dominion.
Under the windings of the sea
They lying long shall not die windily;
Twisting on racks when sinews give way,
Strapped to a wheel, yet they shall not break;
Faith in their hands shall snap in two,
And the unicorn evils run them through;
Split all ends up they shan't crack;
And death shall have no dominion.

And death shall have no dominion.
No more may gulls cry at their ears
Or waves break loud on the seashores;
Where blew a flower may a flower no more
Lift its head to the blows of the rain;
Though they be mad and dead as nails
Heads of the characters hammer through daisies;
Break in the sun till the sun breaks down,
And death shall have no dominion.

Dylan Thomas (1914 – 1953)

Staring Out the Window Three Weeks After His Death

On the last day of his life as he lay comatose in the hospital bed
I saw that his soul was a hare which was poised
In the long grass of his body, ears pricked.
It sprang toward me and halted and I wondered if it
Could hear me breathing
Or if it could smell my own fear which was,
Could he but have known it, greater than his
For plainly he was a just and playful man
And just and playful men are as brave as they are rare.
Then his cancer-eroded body appeared to shudder
As if a gust of wind blew through the long grass
And the hare of his soul made a u-turn
And began bounding away from me
Until it disappeared from sight into a dark wood
And I thought – that is the end of that,
I will not be seeing him again.
He died in front of me, no one else was in the room.
My eyes teemed with tears, I could not damp them down.
I stood up to walk around his bed
Only to catch sight again of the hare of his soul
Springing out of the wood into a beachy cove of sunlight
And I thought – yes, that's how it is going to be from now on:
The hare of his soul always there, when I least expect it;
Popping up out of nowhere, sitting still.

Paul Durcan

Everything is Going to Be All Right

How should I not be glad to contemplate
the clouds clearing beyond the dormer window
and a high tide reflected on the ceiling?
There will be dying, there will be dying,
but there is no need to go into that.
The lines flow from the hand unbidden
and the hidden source is the watchful heart;
the sun rises in spite of everything
and the far cities are beautiful and bright.
I lie here in a riot of sunlight
watching the day break and the clouds flying.
Everything is going to be all right.

Derek Mahon

The Parting Glass

Oh all the time that e'er I spent,
I spent it in good company;
And any harm that e'er I've done,
I trust it was to none but me;
May those I've loved through all the years
Have memories now they'll e'er recall;
So fill to me the parting glass,
Goodnight, and joy be with you all.

Oh all the comrades that e'er I had,
Are sorry for my going away;
And all the loved ones that e'er I had
Would wish me one more day to stay.
But since it falls unto my lot
That I should leave and you should not,
I'll gently rise and I'll softly call
Goodnight, and joy be with you all.

Of all good times that e'er we shared,
I leave to you fond memory;
And for all the friendship that e'er we had
I ask you to remember me;
And when you sit and stories tell,
I'll be with you and help recall;
So fill to me the parting glass,
God bless, and joy be with you all.

Traditional Irish

For Ever and Ever
and for Nuala and Simon

He wanted to be piggybacked the last few hundred yards.
'Wait till we're nearer home.' 'But it's so far!'

I asked if he remembered his grandmother's sister
who died last year. 'Nuala. Yes, I loved her.'

And did he know, every day, in her eighties, she'd walk
down to the café? 'On her own?' 'Of course.'

'And now', he said, 'she has gone away forever...'
'That's right.' But he hadn't finished: '...and ever and ever...'

And so on, all the way home, not at all sadly,
as if by chanting, hitting the same key,

he could turn something, or roll into place some stone
I might want to roll aside and carry him home.

Mark Granier

Death Is Smaller Than I Thought

My Mother and Father died some years ago
I loved them very much.
When they died my love for them
Did not vanish or fade away.
It stayed just about the same,
Only a sadder colour.
And I can feel their love for me,
Same as it ever was.

Nowadays, in good times or bad,
I sometimes ask my Mother and Father
To walk beside me or to sit with me
So we can talk together
Or be silent.

They always come to me.
I talk to them and listen to them
And think I hear them talk to me.
It's very simple –
Nothing to do with spiritualism
Or religion or mumbo jumbo.

It is imaginary.
It is real.
It is love.

Adrian Mitchell (1932 – 2008)

Darling

You might forget the exact sound of her voice
or how her face looked when sleeping.
You might forget the sound of her quiet weeping
curled into the shape of a half moon,

when smaller than her self, she seemed already to be leaving
before she left, when the blossom was on the trees
and the sun was out, and all seemed good in the world.
I held her hand and sang a song from when I was a girl –

Heel y'ho boys, let her go boys –
and when I stopped singing she had slipped away,
already a slip of a girl again, skipping off,
her heart light, her face almost smiling.

And what I didn't know or couldn't say then
was that she hadn't really gone.
The dead don't go till you do, loved ones.
The dead are still here holding our hands.

Jackie Kay

Dirge without Music

I am not resigned to the shutting away of loving hearts in the
    hard ground.
So it is, and so it will be, for so it has been, time out of mind:
Into the darkness they go, the wise and the lovely. Crowned
With lilies and with laurel they go; but I am not resigned.

Lovers and thinkers, into the earth with you.
Be one with the dull, the indiscriminate dust.
A fragment of what you felt, of what you knew,
A formula, a phrase remains, - but the best is lost.

The answers quick & keen, the honest look, the laughter, the
    love, -
They are gone. They are gone to feed the roses. Elegant and
    curled
Is the blossom. Fragrant is the blossom. I know. But I do not
    approve.
More precious was the light in your eyes than all the roses of the
    world.

Down, down, down into the darkness of the grave
Gently they go, the beautiful, the tender, the kind;
Quietly they go, the intelligent, the witty, the brave
I know. But I do not approve. And I am not resigned.

Edna St. Vincent Millay (1892 – 1950)

My Funeral

I hope I can trust you, friends, not to use our relationship
As an excuse for an unsolicited ego-trip.
I have seen enough of them at funerals and they make
   me cross.
At this one, though deceased, I aim to be the boss.
If you are asked to talk about me for five minutes, please
   do not go on for eight.
There is a strict timetable at the crematorium and nobody
   wants to be late.
If invited to read a poem, just read the bloody poem.
   If requested
To sing a song, just sing it, as suggested,
And don't say anything. Though I will not be there,
Glancing pointedly at my watch and fixing the speaker
   with a malevolent stare,
Remember that this was how I always reacted
When I felt that anybody's speech, sermon or poetry reading
   was becoming too protracted.
Yes, I was impatient and intolerant, and not always polite
And if there aren't many people at my funeral, it will
   serve me right.

Wendy Cope

Funeral Blues

Stop all the clocks, cut off the telephone,
Prevent the dog from barking with a juicy bone,
Silence the pianos and with muffled drum
Bring out the coffin, let the mourners come.

Let aeroplanes circle moaning overhead
Scribbling on the sky the message He Is Dead,
Put crêpe bows round the white necks of the public doves,
Let the traffic policemen wear black cotton gloves.

He was my North, my South, my East and West,
My working week and my Sunday rest,
My noon, my midnight, my talk, my song;
I thought that love would last for ever: I was wrong.

The stars are not wanted now: put out every one;
Pack up the moon and dismantle the sun;
Pour away the ocean and sweep up the wood.
For nothing now can ever come to any good.

W. H. Auden (1907 – 1973)

Funeral Song from *Cymbeline*

Fear no more the heat o' th' sun,
  Nor the furious winter's rages,
Thou thy worldly task has done,
  Home art gone and ta'en thy wages.
Golden lads and girls all must,
As chimney-sweepers, come to dust.

Fear no more the frown o' th' great,
  Thou art past the tyrant's stroke
Care no more to clothe and eat,
  To thee the reed is as the oak:
The sceptre, learning, physic, must
All follow this and come to dust.

Fear no more the lightning-flash.
  Nor th' all-dreaded thunder-stone.
Fear not slander, censure rash.
  Thou hast finish'd joy and moan.
All lovers young, all lovers must
Consign to thee and come to dust.

No exorciser harm thee!
Nor no witchcraft charm thee!
Ghost unlaid forbear thee!
Nothing ill come near thee!
Quiet consummation have,
And renowned be thy grave!

William Shakespeare (1564 – 1616)

Crossing the Bar

Sunset and evening star,
  And one clear call for me!
And may there be no moaning of the bar,
  When I put out to sea,

But such a tide as moving seems asleep,
  Too full for sound and foam,
When that which drew from out the boundless deep
  Turns again home.

Twilight and evening bell,
  And after that the dark!
And may there be no sadness of farewell,
  When I embark;

For tho' from out our bourne of Time and Place
  The flood may bear me far,
I hope to see my Pilot face to face
  When I have crost the bar.

Alfred, Lord Tennyson (1809 – 1892)

The Scattering

I cast you into the waters.
Be lake, or random moon.

Be first light,
lifting up its beggar's cup.

I scatter your ashes.
Be the gale teaching autumn
to mend its ways,
or leopard so proud of his spotted coat.

Be the mentor of cherry trees.

I cast your dust far and wide,
a sower broadcasting seed:
Be wild rose or hellebore or all-heal.

Descend as a vein of silver,
never to be seen,
deep in the lynx-eyed earth.

Rise as barn owl white as dusk;
dove or raven marvelling at his flight.
Know different delights.

Penelope Shuttle

Epitaph on a Friend

An honest man here lies at rest,
The friend of man, the friend of truth,
The friend of age, and guide of youth:
Few hearts like his, with virtue warm'd,
Few heads with knowledge so inform'd;
If there's another world, he lives in bliss;
If there is none, he made the best of this.

Robert Burns (1759 – 1796)

Ode to My Brother

By ways remote and distant waters sped,
Brother, to thy sad grave-side am I come,
That I may give the last gifts to the dead
And vainly parley with thine ashes dumb;
Since she who now bestows and now denies
Hath taken thee, hapless brother, from mine eyes.

But lo! these gifts, the heirlooms of past years,
Are made sad things to grace thy coffin shell,
Take them, all drenched with a brother's tears,
And, brother, for all time, hail and farewell.

Catullus (c.84 – c.54 BC)

In Flanders Fields

In Flanders fields the poppies blow
Between the crosses, row on row,
That mark our place; and in the sky
The larks, still bravely singing, fly
Scarce heard amid the guns below.

We are the Dead. Short days ago
We lived, felt dawn, saw sunset glow,
Loved and were loved, and now we lie
In Flanders fields.

Take up our quarrel with the foe:
To you from failing hands we throw
The torch; be yours to hold it high.
If ye break faith with us who die
We shall not sleep, though poppies grow
In Flanders fields.

Lieutenant-Colonel John McCrae (1872 – 1918)

from 'For The Fallen'

They shall not grow old, as we that are left grow old:
    Age shall not weary them, nor the years condemn.
At the going down of the sun and in the morning
    We will remember them.

Laurence Binyon (1869 – 1943)

Vanished

She died, - this was the way she died;
And when her breath was done,
Took up her simple wardrobe
And started for the sun.

Her little figure at the gate
The angels must have spied,
Since I could never find her
Upon the mortal side.

Emily Dickinson (1830 - 1886)

Prayer

Let us be ears for the end of grass
the flickering, whispering grass,
the purple seeds carried like snow
beneath pylons, behind piers,
in late August or dry September.

Let us be mouths for the falling wind
thrumming, howling, then singing
through old fences and fairgrounds,
and in the first light let us be near
the stalled, the stuttering heart.

Let us be blessed in this house
with its emptinesses, its emptinesses —
let us attend to the passing
of small things: the lost nail,
the dropped stitch, the one pearl.

Faith Lawrence

Spring and Grief

I see my love in every little child
Whose eyes meet mine with laughter in their blue;
I hear him in the note, half sweet, half wild,
When bird calls bird their promise to renew;
I feel him in the ardor of the sun
That woos the fragrance from the waking flower,
And maple buds, rose flushed by beauty, won
To swift fulfilment of the Sun God's power.
The world is young once more as he was young,
With life and love reborn in everything –
O singing hearts! My own is faint and wrung;
The rapture and the riot of the Spring
Can but enhance the throb of my despair –
I miss him most when joy is everywhere!

Corinne Roosevelt Robinson (1861 – 1933)

Epitaph on a Child

Here, freed from pain, secure from misery, lies
A child, the darling of his parents' eyes;
A gentler lamb ne'er sported on the plain,
A fairer flower will never bloom again.
Few were the days allotted to his breath;
Now let him sleep in peace his night of death.

Thomas Gray (1716 – 1771)

Pink

white horses still their clattering feet
and wait for you
in shadow street their pink-plumed heads
stand straight for you
the lady at the bus-stop signs
a cross for you
the walker with the terrier dog
sighs loss for you
the traffic at the roundabout
must queue for you
the metronome of trotting hooves
beats true for you
the wagons on the carriageway
change gears for you
the rider on the cycle-path
wipes tears for you
pink rose-bay and foxgloves paint
July for you
the sunlight on the fell pours down
goodbye for you
the smiles of all who met you weave
the pall for you
that pink box in a white hearse is
too small for you
a sailing group of pink balloons
learn flight with you
and high the wings of wheeling birds
delight with you

Sue Millard

Eulogy

Warm summer sun
  shine kindly here,
Warm Southern wind
  blow softly here,
Green sod above
  lie light, lie light –
Good night, dear heart,
  good night, good night.

Mark Twain (1835 – 1910) after Robert Richardson

Published by:
Candlestick Press,
Diversity House, 72 Nottingham Road,
Arnold, Nottingham NG5 6LF
www.candlestickpress.co.uk

Design, typesetting, print and production by Diversity Creative
Marketing Solutions Ltd., www.diversitymarketing.co.uk

Introduction © Carol Ann Duffy, 2012

Illustrations © Lizzie Adcock, www.arumliliedesigns.co.uk

© Candlestick Press, 2012

First Published 2012
Reprinted 2014

ISBN 978 1 907598 15 9

Acknowledgements:
Our thanks to the Poet Laureate, Carol Ann Duffy, for her support.
Thanks are due to Lorraine Mariner for her researches. Thanks are also
due to the authors, publishers and agents below for permission to
reprint the following:

Christopher Reid, excerpt from 'Lucinda's Way' from *A Scattering*,
Areté Books, 2009, is reprinted by kind permission of the author;
Peter Porter, excerpt from 'An Exequy' from *The Rest on the Flight:
Selected Poems*, 2010, is reprinted by kind permission of Pan
Macmillian, London. Copyright © Peter Porter, 2010; Dylan Thomas,
'And Death Shall Have No Dominion' is reprinted from *Collected
Poems*, Orion, 2000; Paul Durcan, 'Staring Out The Window Three
Weeks After His Death' from *Praise In Which I Live And Move And
Have My Being*, Harvill Secker, 2012, is reprinted by kind permission
of the author and was first published in *Poetry London*; Derek Mahon,
'Everything is Going to Be All Right' is reprinted by kind permission
of the author and The Gallery Press, Loughcrew, Oldcastle, County
Meath, Ireland from *New Collected Poems* (2011); Mark Granier,
'For Ever And Ever' is printed by kind permission of the author;
Adrian Mitchell, 'Death Is Smaller Than I Thought' from *In Person:
30 Poets*, Bloodaxe Books, 2008, is reprinted by permission of United
Agents on behalf of The Estate of Adrian Mitchell; Jackie Kay,
'Darling' is reprinted from *Darling: New and Selected Poems*,
Bloodaxe Books, 2007; Wendy Cope, 'My Funeral' is reprinted from
Family Values, Faber and Faber Ltd, 2011; W H Auden, 'Funeral Blues'
is from *Another Time*, Random House, 1940. Copyright © 1940 by

W H Auden, renewed. Reprinted by permission of Curtis Brown, Ltd; Carol Ann Duffy, 'Cold', from *The Bees*, Picador, 2010, is reprinted by kind permission of the author; Billy Collins, 'The Dead' is reprinted from *Taking Off Emily Dickinson's Clothes*, Picador, 2000, reprinted by kind permission of Pan Macmillan, London. Copyright © Billy Collins, 2000; Anna Wigley, 'The Baton' is reprinted from *Waking in Winter*, Gomer Press, 2009; Penelope Shuttle, 'The Scattering', is reprinted from *Sandgrain and Hourglass*, Bloodaxe Books, 2010; Extract from "Carrying the Elephant: A Memoir of Love and Loss" by Michael Rosen (© Michael Rosen, 2002) is reproduced by permission of United Agents (www.unitedagents.co.uk) on behalf of Michael Rosen; Faith Lawrence, 'Prayer', is printed by kind permission of the author; Sue Millard, 'Pink' is reprinted by kind permission of the author and is in memory of Naomi Bernard (2005 – 2011). It first appeared in *The Interpreter's House*; Laurence Binyon, excerpt from 'For The Fallen' is reprinted by permission of The Society of Authors as the Literary Representative of the Estate of Laurence Binyon.

Where poets are no longer living, their dates are given.